BOOK ANALYSIS

Written by

Transla

Silk

BY ALESSANDRO BARICCO

BrightSummaries.com

ALESSANDRO BARICCO

ITALIAN WRITER, COMPOSER, PRODUCER AND DIRECTOR

- **Born in Turin in 1958**
- **Notable works:**
    - *Lands of Glass* (1991), novel
    - *Novecento* (1994), novel
    - *Silk* (1996), novel

Alessandro Baricco is an Italian writer, composer, producer and director, and was born in Turin in 1958. His first novel, *Land of Glass* (published in Italian in 1991), received France's *Prix Médicis étranger* in 1995. He published *Novecento*, a theatrical monologue, in 1994. Two years later, with *Silk*, he established himself as one of the major writers of the new generation. He currently contributes to the Italian daily newspaper *La Repubblica* and teaches at the Scuola Holden, a school of narrative techniques which he founded with his friends.

SILK

A LOVE STORY SHROUDED IN MYSTERY

- **Genre:** novel
- **Reference edition:** Baricco, A. (2006) *Silk*. Trans. Goldstein, A. Edinburgh: Canongate.
- **First edition:** 1996
- **Themes:** silkworm farming, travel, Japan, mystery, love, nostalgia

Silk (*Seta* in Italian) is Alessandro Baricco's third novel. When it was published in 1996 it became a bestseller in Italy, where it has sold over 300 000 copies to date. It has been translated into 27 languages and first appeared in English in 1997, with a second translation by Ann Goldstein published in 2006.

The story immerses the reader in the heart of the silkworm trade in the 19th century: following an epidemic which infects silkworms all over Europe, Hervé Joncour undertakes four journeys to Japan to buy healthy eggs and allow his village to continue in the silk trade. These journeys lead him towards a strange romantic destiny. Baricco gives us a work that is all silence, restraint and refinement, marked by a very distinctive writing style. The book is similar to the life of its hero: a "spectacle. Light and inexplicable" (p. 136).

SUMMARY

In 1861, Hervé Joncour is 32 years old and lives in Lavilledieu, in the Midi region of France, with his wife Hélène. His profession is unusual: he buys and sells silkworm eggs. To do this, he goes to Egypt and Syria for several months each year and comes back with the goods; the rest of the time, he relaxes. However, that year an epidemic of pébrine (a silkworm disease caused by a fungus) breaks out all over the world, and all the silkworm eggs are infected. Baldabiou, the man who set up the silkworm farm in Lavilledieu and built the first spinning mill, suggests a solution: going to Japan. The island has been closed to foreigners for a long time which, according to him, guarantees that the epidemic will not have reached it. The silkworm farmers therefore decide to send Hervé Joncour to Japan. He leaves on the 6 October.

After a long journey, he arrives in the country and tries to buy silkworm eggs, but he is given fish eggs, which he notices straight away. As he is leaving, one of the residents catches him and tells him that Hara Kei, a nobleman of the village, wants to see him. Accompanied by a mysterious young girl, Hara Kei receives Hervé Joncour and asks him who he is. The Frenchman then tells him the story of his life, but is nevertheless somewhat troubled by the young girl, whose identity Hara Kei refuses to reveal to him: "what he saw, without pausing, was that those eyes did not have an Oriental shape, and that they were fixed, with a disconcerting intensity, on him" (p. 30). He still does not know that his entire life will be marked by the nostalgic memory of this unknown girl.

Once he has finished telling his story, Hara Kei tells him that he has been sold fish eggs, but that now he can have what he wants. With the real eggs, Hervé Joncour travels back and arrives in Lavilledieu on the first day of April. The eggs he has brought back are healthy, which enables a very good output of silk that year.

The following year, during another journey to Japan, the silkworm farmer is bathing one day when, instead of the old women who usually wash him, a young girl arrives. She blindfolds him and brushes his lips with her hand, before giving him a note which has several ideograms drawn on it in black ink. This message troubles him, especially when he returns to Lavilledieu and learns its meaning thanks to Madame Blanche, a Japanese woman living in Nîmes: "Return, or I will die" (p. 58).

After returning to France, he tries to go back to his normal life but he cannot stop himself from thinking about the young girl he met in Japan. However, for the first time Hervé Joncour takes his wife Hélène on holiday to Nice and tells her that he will always love her.

In spite of an imminent civil war in Japan, Baldabiou asks Hervé Joncour to go back there. Hervé Joncour therefore leaves at the start of October. When he arrives to see Hara Kei, he finds the young girl in front of the aviary. She greets him in French, while the nobleman tells him that she does not understand the language. One evening, when he is returning to his lodgings after a party, Hervé Joncour meets her, accompanied by an Oriental woman. She places his hand on the other woman's and runs away, leaving them to share a night of passion. The next day, Hara Kei has disappeared and none of his servants know when he will return. Hervé Joncour waits another two days, then leaves the village and goes back to Lavilledieu to see his wife. Once there, he becomes ill and makes sure not to see anyone. From July to September, he and his wife leave to go to Nice.

One year later, war has broken out in Japan. Surprisingly, Hervé Joncour goes against Baldabiou's opinion and insists on going there in spite of everything. Baldabiou questions Hervé Joncour about his real reason for wanting to make the journey and Hervé Joncour tells him everything. He has not forgotten the young girl. It is a particular kind of suffering: he is nostalgic for something he has not experienced, since he has never heard her voice. Hélène, who understands that her husband is the one who absolutely wants to return to Japan, makes him promise to come back.

When Hervé Joncour arrives in Hara Kei's village, he finds the place devastated. The only person he meets is a young boy who guides him, after several wordless days of walking, to the villagers, who are fleeing in a long procession. But Hara Kei is not happy to see Hervé Joncour and orders him to leave. The Frenchman does not see the young girl, but surmises that she is in a sedan chair adorned with cages containing birds. In the morning, he finds his guide dead. Hara Kei threatens him with a gun and explains to him that the boy has been killed because he was carrying, or rather was himself a message of love, which in Japan is one of twelve crimes for which a man can be sentenced to death. He orders Hervé Joncour to never comes back.

Hervé Joncour manages to buy eggs, but they die before he reaches Lavilledieu. Then, to give the village work in spite of the lack of eggs and therefore of silk, he takes on all the men for four months to work on the park around his house.

Six months later he receives a letter in Japanese which he hurries to have translated by Madame Blanche. He is evidently convinced that it was sent by the young girl he met in Japan. However, it was actually sent by his wife, who was helped by Madame Blanche to translate it into Japanese. It is a love and farewell letter. Following this, Hervé Joncour continues to live peacefully with his wife. They now go on a little journey every year. In March 1874, Hélène dies. When he visits her grave, Hervé Joncour finds a ring with blue flowers on it similar to the one worn by Madame Blanche. He goes to see her and then understands that it was Hélène who wrote him the letter.

Hervé Joncour lives another 23 years without ever leaving Lavilledieu again, and dedicates all his time to the upkeep of his park.

CHARACTER STUDY

HERVÉ JONCOUR

He is 32 years old at the start of the story. He is the novel's main character. He lives in Lavilledieu, in the Midi region of France, with his wife Hélène. They have no children. They are neither happy nor unhappy. He is presented as a calm, indifferent and passive man: "He was, besides, one of those men who like to *witness* their own life, considering any ambition to *live* it inappropriate" (p. 7). He lets himself be guided by Baldabiou, who dictates his life choices for him: his profession and his departure for Japan. He only really asserts himself on one occasion: he insists on going to Japan after the war has broken out.

In Japan, Hervé Joncour meets a mysterious young girl. Disconcerted by her eyes, he falls in love with her while knowing almost nothing about her. When he returns from his travels, he sensibly tries to return to his normal life, but he cannot get the young girl and her mysteries out of his mind. It is a love that gives rise to suffering in him: he feels nostalgic for something that he has not completely known in reality.

HÉLÈNE

Hélène is Hervé Joncour's wife. "She was a tall woman, she moved slowly, she had long black hair that she never gathered on to her head. She had a beautiful voice" (p. 23).

Great gentleness and profound humility emerge from this somewhat unassuming character: each time her husband returns, she welcomes him with extreme tenderness, forcing herself not to cry despite her worries. The letter that she sends to Hervé Joncour is tremendous proof of her love. Ultimately she is the one who in a way holds the key to the story.

She is also very attached to Baldabiou: normally so reserved, she cries when he leaves the village.

BALDABIOU

Baldabiou is presented in a way as the wise man of the village: he knows everything ("Baldabiou knew all these stories", p. 21). It is thanks to him that Lavilledieu has become an important centre for silk production. He also plays a major role in Hervé Joncour's life: he encouraged him to go into trade while his father wanted him to dedicate himself to a great military career (when Hervé Joncour's father says "My son Hervé, who in two days will return to Paris, where a brilliant career awaits him in our army, God and St Agnes willing", Baldabiou responds "Exactly. Only, God is busy elsewhere and St Agnes detests soldiers", p. 14). He is also the one who sends Hervé Joncour to Japan. Futhermore, Hervé Joncour seems to always follow his advice: "he was letting this man methodically rewrite his destiny" (p. 17). There is only one exception to this: when war breaks out in Japan and Baldabiou wants to stop Hervé Joncour from going there, the latter opposes him and leaves in spite of the risks he is exposing himself to.

Baldabiou is an original character with a strong personality. A lover of billiards, he spends his time playing it alone, against himself, in the back room of a café. He acts as if there were two players, one good ("the normal man") and one bad ("the one-armed player"). He says that the day that the "one-armed player" wins the match, he will leave the city (p. 53). This will be the thing that determines his departure, after living in Lavilledieu for years: when, "On June 16, 1871, in the back of Verdun's café, before noon, the one-armed player made an irrational four-cushion draw shot" (p. 137), Baldabiou leaves the city.

THE YOUNG GIRL

The young girl who Hervé Joncour meets in Japan is shrouded in mystery. As soon as he sees her, he notices that "those eyes did not have an Oriental shape" (p. 30). However, when he talks about her to an Englishman he meets, the latter tells him that there are no white women in Japan (p. 44). Likewise, the young girl talks to him in French while Hara Kei, a minute later, states that she does not know the language.

It can be supposed that she is Hara Kei's wife or daughter, but nothing is said explicitly. In any case, he protects her and does not seem to want to share her: it is because of the exchange of the message of love that Hara Kei orders Hervé Joncour to not come back.

HARA KEI

Hara Kei is a powerful man. He seems to have a great presence and controls all the arrivals of strangers in his village: the first time Hervé Joncour comes to the region to buy eggs, at first he is only given false eggs; it is only after he has met with Hara Kei that he can receive the real goods. It is said of him that "As if by a special rule, wherever that man went, he went in an unconditional and perfect solitude" (p. 46).

ANALYSIS

THE DECLINE OF SILKWORM FARMING IN FRANCE

Baricco sets his narrative in the context of the silkworm trade in 1861. At that time Lavilledieu was a major centre for sericulture (the farming of silkworms, which are the caterpillars of the *Bombyx mori* butterfly; their cocoons provide the silk). This craft had a substantial presence in France until 1860. Then, following the development of epidemics which decimated the silkworm population, the production of cocoons was almost exclusively confined to Asia.

As the author refers to a real economic and historical context, *Silk* can in a way be considered to be a historical novel. The main characteristic of this genre is that it takes real events as its backdrop and combines them with fictional events and characters. Here, the protagonists are straight from the writer's imagination.

THE ART OF COPY AND PASTE

Alessandro Baricco's text is littered with identical passages which give rhythm to the narrative:

- For example, the historical context is described in exactly the same way, almost to the word, twice: "It was 1861. Flaubert was writing/finishing Salammbô, electric light was still a hypothesis and Abraham Lincoln, on the other side of the ocean, was fighting a war whose end he would not see" (pp. 1 and 23).

- Likewise, each journey towards Japan is narrated in a similar way, almost word for word (Chapters 12, 19, 31 and 34).
- The first three returns from Japan are also narrated almost identically (Chapters 17, 24 and 38).
- Finally, the same phrase is used each time Hervé Joncour sees the young girl: "Her eyes did not have an Oriental shape, and her face was the face of a girl" (pp. 30, 40 and 69).

These passages offer points of reference for the reader and allow the author to quickly pass over the journeys to concentrate on several days, a particular moment or even a look that is exchanged.

WRITING WHERE FORM IS LINKED TO CONTENT

With its simple, light and poetic writing, *Silk* seems to imitate the delicate refinement of Japanese calligraphy: "Baldabiou said that they came from Paris, sometimes, to make love with Madame Blanche. Returning to the capital, they displayed on the lapel of their evening jacket little blue flowers, the ones she always wore on her fingers, as if they were rings" (p. 59). This calligraphy itself is central to the novel because it is the coded language of the message of love from the young girl and the long love letter written by Hélène.

The gentleness of this short narrative can also be compared

to the gentleness of silk, a material which is also central to the work, and more specifically to Hervé Joncour's initial quest. As such, thanks to the writing style, form and content are in perfect harmony.

"A SPECTACLE. LIGHT AND INEXPLICABLE"

The expression used by Baricco to describe how Hervé Joncour perceives his own life (see the last words of the novel, p. 148: "the inexplicable spectacle, light, that had been his life") can also be applied to the novel as a whole. Like poetry (some very short chapters also resemble poems, such as Chapters 29 and 48), the narrative only touches feelings or events with its fingertips, without really saying them or giving an explanation. For example, Hervé Joncour's obsessive love for the young girl is impalpable and Hélène's love for her husband, apart from in the letter, appears more in a diffuse gentleness than in specific words or actions. In this way, the author leaves a great deal of room for the reader's imagination.

FURTHER REFLECTION

SOME QUESTIONS TO THINK ABOUT...

- How would you sum up the message of this book in a single sentence?
- Describe the psychological evolution of Hervé Joncour.
- If you were to make this novel into a film, what kind of music would you use for its soundtrack?
- It can be said that the novel, like the life of its hero, is "A spectacle. Light and inexplicable". Explain why.
- Can Hervé Joncour be considered to have been unfaithful to his wife Hélène? Justify your point of view.
- The young girl whom Hervé Joncour meets in Japan is somewhat mysterious. What does the protagonist really know about her? Describe their relationship.
- Do you think Hervé Joncour really fell in love? With who or what?
- How could the friendship between the hero and Baldabiou be characterised?
- Baricco's text includes several passages which are almost identical word for word. Why do you think the author has done this?
- What are the main themes which are developed in this novel?

We want to hear from you!
Leave a comment on your online library
and share your favourite books on social media!

FURTHER READING

REFERENCE EDITION

- Baricco, A. (2006) *Silk*. Trans. Goldstein, A. Edinburgh: Canongate.

ADAPTATIONS

- *Silk* (2009) [Film]. François Girard. Dir. Canada/United Kingdom/Japan: New Line Cinema.

www.brightsummaries.com

Ebook EAN: 9782806287908

Paperback EAN: 9782806290472

Legal Deposit: D/2016/12603/815

Cover: © Primento

Digital conception by Primento, the digital partner of publishers.

29390360R00016

Printed in Great Britain
by Amazon